Maasai

Maasai

🇬🇧

*O*f Africa's many tribes and cultures, the Maasai, perhaps
more so than any other, have captured the imagination of
writers and adventurers. They have struggled to maintain a
special relationship with their land and cattle, and have protected
a culture against the pressures of the modern age. The pastoral
Maasai are part of a larger grouping of peoples who speak the
Maa language and live in southern Kenya and northern
Tanzania. Some are now farmers, workers and professionals,
others have remained attached to their pastoral traditions and
still live in Maasailand in the thorn-branch surrounded home-
stead called the enkang. Large herds of cattle, and smaller herds
of goats and sheep, are penned inside the thorn stockade at night
to protect them from predators. Young boys are soon taught to
herd the prized cattle, sometimes within view of the lofty summit
of Africa's highest peak, Kilimanjaro.

🇩🇪

*V*on allen Stämmen und Kulturen Afrikas haben die Massai
wohl die größte Faszination auf Schriftsteller und Abenteu-
rer ausgeübt. Sie haben sich sehr darum bemüht, ihr besonderes
Verhältnis zu ihrem Land und ihrem Vieh zu bewahren, und
haben ihre Kultur gegen den Einfluß des modernen Zeitalters
geschützt. Die pastoralen Massai sind Teil einer größeren Stam-
mesgruppierung, in der man die Sprache Maa spricht. Sie leben
in Südkenia und Nordtansania. Einige Massai wurden Farmer,
oder Berufstätige, andere wiederum blieben ihren pastoralen Traditionen treu und leben noch heute in ihren Siedlungen, Enkang,
im Massailand. Große Rinderherden und kleinere Ziegen- und
Schafherden werden nachts in den dornenumzäunten Einfrie-
dungen vor Raubtieren geschützt. Die kleinen Massaijungen lernen schon früh – vor der beeindruckenden Kulisse des Kilimand-
scharo, Afrikas höchstem Berg – das wertvolle Vieh zu hüten.

🇫🇷

*D*es nombreuses tribus et cultures d'Afrique, ce sont sans
aucun doute les Maasais qui ont le plus frappé l'imagination
des écrivains et des chercheurs d'aventure. Les hommes maasais
se sont efforcés de préserver les rapports spéciaux qu'ils ont avec
leurs terres et leur bétail, et ont sauvegardé leur culture malgré
les influences de l'ère moderne. Les Maasais font partie d'un
groupe étendu de tribus parlant la langue maa, vivant dans le
sud du Kenya et dans le nord de la Tanzanie. Certains sont
devenus agriculteurs, employés ou membres des professions
libérales; les autres sont restés attachés à la terre et continuent à
vivre en Maasailand dans leurs enkangs, fermes protegées par
une enceinte d'épineux. De grands troupeaux de bétail, ainsi que
des troupeaux plus petits de chèvres et de moutons sont enfermés
pendant la nuit dans ces enclos entourés d'épineux afin de les
protéger des animaux sauvages. Les garçons maasais apprennent
très jeune à garder le précieux bétail de tribu, souvent en vue du
plus haut sommet d'Afrique: le Kilimandjaro.

🇬🇧   *Two things are valued by the Maasai above all else: children and cattle. In the Maa language spoken by the Maasai, the common greeting 'Keserian ingera? Keserian ingishu?' means 'How are the children? How are the cattle?' Parents devote a great deal of time to caring for young children (below). A close bond exists between Maasai mothers and their infants. Babies are often adorned with bead necklaces or waistbands (opposite), mirroring the ornate beads and necklaces worn by their mothers. For the first six years of childhood Maasai children spend much of the day at play. Boys begin to learn how to herd cattle and goats by pretending to be herdsmen (left).*

🇩🇪   *Die wertvollsten Dinge im Leben eines Massai sind seine Kinder und Viehherden. In der Maa-Sprache der Massai lautet der häufigste Gruß: "Keserian ingera? Keserian ingishu?", was soviel bedeutet wie: "Wie geht es den Kindern? Wie geht es dem Vieh?" Eltern widmen ihren kleinen Kindern viel Aufmerksamkeit und Zuwendung (unten). Zwischen den Massaimüttern und ihren Kindern besteht ein besonders enges Band. Die Mütter, die kunstvolle Perlenornamente und Ketten tragen, schmücken auch oft ihre Kleinkinder mit Perlenketten oder -gürteln (rechts). Während der ersten sechs Jahre ihres Lebens verbringen die Massaikinder die meiste Zeit mit Spielen. So lernen die kleinen Massaijungen auch im Spiel, wie man Rinder und Ziegen hüten muß – ein wichtiger Lernprozeß für die zukünftigen Hirten (links).*

🇫🇷   *Les enfants et le bétail sont pour les Maasais les deux choses les plus précieuses. Dans leur langue, le maa, la salutation courante est: 'Keserian ingera? Keserian ingishu?' signifiant 'Comment vont les enfants?' et 'Comment va le bétail?' Les parents passent beaucoup de temps à s'occuper des jeunes enfants (ci-dessous). Mères et enfants maasais sont très attachés l'un à l'autre. Les bébés sont souvent parés de ceintures ou de colliers (ci-contre) semblables à ceux portés par leurs mères. Durant leurs six premières années, les jeunes Maasais passent la plus grande partie de leur temps à jouer. Les garçons apprennent à garder le bétail et les chèvres en jouant au gardien de troupeau (à gauche).*

A young child contemplates the world from the entrance of a dung-plastered dwelling within the enkang (above left). *Boys are taught to care for young animals, such as a baby goat* (right), *while girls are sent out to gather sticks, and assist with cooking, milking and cleaning chores. A young girl, or* entito (above right), *lugs home a grass mat, or* esos, *used to pen infant animals within the comfort of a dwelling. Beaded necklaces are worn only by the girls* (opposite), *but both boys and girls sport enlarged ear lobes.*

Ein Kind betrachtet durch die Hüttentür die Welt in der Enkang (oben links). *Den Jungen wird gezeigt, wie sie sich um Tierjunge, wie z.B. ein Zicklein kümmern müssen* (rechts), *während die Mädchen Zweige sammeln und beim Kochen, Melken und Putzen mithelfen. Ein junges Mädchen, auch* Entito *genannt (oben rechts), schleppt eine Strohmatte,* Esos, *nach Hause, um damit in einer Hütte innerhalb der* Enkang *Jungtiere einzupferchen. Nur Mädchen schmücken sich mit Perlenketten (gegenüber), doch sowohl Jungen als auch Mädchen haben durchbrochene Ohrläppchen.*

Un jeune enfant observe le monde par l'entrée d'une hutte (ci-dessus, à gauche). Les garçons apprennent à prendre soin des jeunes animaux, tel que ce chevreau (à droite); les filles ramassent du bois, aident à préparer les repas, font la traite et le nettoyage. Une jeune fille, ou entito *(ci-dessus, à droite), transporte une natte, ou* esos, *employée pour enclore les jeunes animaux à l'abri, à l'intérieur des habitations. Les colliers ne sont portés que par les filles (ci-contre), mais filles aussi bien que garçons arborent des oreilles aux lobes allongés.*

In Maasai society circumcision is a ritual that signifies the passing of childhood. Once boys have been circumcised, they graduate to become moran, new recruits to the rank of warrior. The ceremony establishes the first age-set in Maasai society. The ceremony has to be planned at least two months in advance. Honey beer is prepared for the ceremony, and the elders arrive to witness the event (above). The boy, usually about 12 years of age, is dressed in a black apron and is decorated with white chalk (opposite top). For several months after the ceremony, the circumcised boys dress in black, paint their faces white, and wear the ostrich feather headdresses (opposite bottom and inset) that indicate their status. The boy who shows no pain brings honour to his parents.

Bei den Massai steht das Ritual der Beschneidung als Symbol für den Ausklang der Kindheit. Sobald ein Junge beschnitten ist, wird aus ihm ein Morani, ein neuer Krieger. Die Zeremonie wird zwei Monate im voraus geplant. Zu diesem Anlaß braut man Honigbier, und die Stammesältesten stellen sich ein, um das Ereignis zu bezeugen (oben). Der rund zwölfjährige Junge wird mit einem schwarzen Schurz bekleidet und mit weißer Kreide bemalt (rechts oben). Noch monatelang nach der Feier kleiden sich die beschnittenen Jungen schwarz, reiben sich die Gesichter weiß ein, tragen einen Kopfschmuck aus Straußenfedern (rechts unten und Einsatz) und weisen damit auf ihren neuen Status hin. Wer keinen Schmerz zeigt, macht seinen Eltern große Ehre.

Dans la culture maasai, la circoncision est le rite qui signifie la fin de l'enfance. Une fois circoncis, les garçons deviennent des moran, ou nouvelles recrues parmi les guerriers. La cérémonie se prépare au moins deux mois à l'avance. On fait de la bière, et les anciens arrivent pour suivre l'événement (ci-dessus). Le garçon, généralement d'une douzaine d'années, est revêtu d'un tablier noir et enduit de craie blanche (ci-contre, en haut). Pendant plusieurs mois après la cérémonie, les garçons circoncis se revêtent de noir, se couvrent le visage de blanc et portent la coiffe de plumes d'autruche (ci-contre, en bas et en cartouche) afin de signaler leur changement de statut. Le garçon qui ne dévoile pas sa souffrance fait honneur à ses parents.

Several days of feasting, drinking and jubilation follow the circumcision (opposite top). Blood is ceremoniously extracted from the neck of a young bull (opposite bottom right) by two moran and a young woman chosen for the occasion. The blood is collected in a gourd, mixed with milk, and given to the circumcised boy to drink. Towards the end of the period of healing, and before they are accepted as junior warriors, the youths prepare circular headdresses decorated with stuffed birds hunted during their sojourn in the bush (below and opposite bottom left).

Der Beschneidung folgt ein mehrtägiges Fest (links). Zwei zu diesem Anlaß ausgewählte Moran sowie eine junge Frau zapfen Blut aus dem Hals eines jungen Stiers (links unten), das in einer Kürbisflasche aufgefangen, mit Milch gemischt und den beschnittenen Jungen zum Trinken gegeben wird. Bevor sie als Jungkrieger anerkannt werden, fertigt sich jeder Heranwachsende einen runden Kopfschmuck an, den er mit Vögeln schmückt, die er während seines Aufenthalts im Busch gejagt und dann ausgestopft hat (unten und ganz links unten).

La circoncision est suivie par plusieurs jours de réjouissances, passés à festoyer (ci-contre, en haut). Du sang est extrait du cou d'un jeune taureau (ci-contre, en bas à droite) par deux moran et une femme spécialement désignés. Le sang est melangé avec du lait et donné au circoncis. Vers la fin de la période de convalescence, et avant qu'ils ne joignent les rangs des jeunes guerriers, les adolescents préparent des coiffes rondes décorées avec des oiseaux empaillés, attrapés à la chasse durant leur séjour en brousse (ci-dessous et ci-contre, en bas à gauche).

With the passing of childhood, the young Maasai men of the age-set graduate to the esteemed ranks of the moran (below). Initially the junior warriors, the ilkeliani (opposite top), live with their parents. The young morani begins to grow his hair and regularly applies red ochre (opposite bottom). Ear lobes are adorned with colourful beads, and a special neckband is worn. After some time, the junior warriors join the senior warriors (inset) to form a single unit in the manyatta, a settlement built to accommodate the moran and their attendants. The moran return from the bush to receive a jubilant welcome (overleaf).

Ist ihre Kindheit abgeschlossen, erhalten die jungen Männer einer Altersgruppe den angesehenen Rang der Moran (unten). Anfangs wohnen die Jungkrieger oder Ilkeliani (rechts) bei ihren Eltern. Der junge Morani läßt sein Haar wachsen und reibt es mit rotem Ocker ein (rechts unten). Die Ohrläppchen werden mit bunten Perlen geschmückt, und er trägt ein besonderes Halsband. Nach einiger Zeit schließen sich die jungen Krieger mit den älteren (Einsatz) in einer Manyatta zusammen, einer Siedlung, die eigens für die Moran und deren Begleiter gebaut wurde. Kommen die Moran aus dem Busch zurück, werden sie freudig begrüßt (umseitig).

Ayant atteint l'âge requis à la fin de l'enfance, les jeunes Maasais sont promus au grade respectable de moran (ci-dessous). Au début, les jeunes guerriers, les ilkeliani (ci-contre, en haut) vivent avec leurs parents. Le jeune morani laisse pousser ses cheveux et les couvre régulièrement d'ocre rouge (ci-contre, en bas). Les lobes des oreilles sont parés de perles, et un bandeau spécial est porté autour du cou. Plus tard, les guerriers rejoignent leurs aînés pour constituer une seule communauté dans le manyatta, un camp établi pour eux (en cartouche). Quand le morani revient de la brousse il reçoit une bienvenue enthousiaste (page suivante).

🇬🇧 *The* moran *share a close kinship and everything is shared. Warriors, according to traditional law in Maasai society, may never eat alone and are always found together in groups (above). During the years spent in the* manyatta, *the* moran *grow their hair and devote much time to plaiting it (opposite bottom left). At close of day, the* moran *often dance the* adumu *jumping dance of the Maasai (opposite bottom right). The dance, as well as the songs that accompany it, recall legendary cattle raids, battles, and the deeds of brave men. Much of the antics of the* moran *are closely watched by young girls (opposite top), while the* moran *for their part pretend not to notice.*

🇩🇪 *Die Krieger fühlen sich eng miteinander verbunden und teilen alles. Die Tradition der Massai erlaubt ihnen nicht, alleine zu essen, und sie bewegen sich immer in Gruppen (oben). Während der Jahre, die die* Moran *in der* Manyatta *zubringen, lassen sie sich die Haare wachsen und flechten und färben diese dann (rechts). Abends tanzen die* Moran *oft den typischen* Adumu-Springtanz *(ganz rechts). Der Tanz, wie auch die begleitenden Lieder rufen Erinnerungen an legendäre Viehdiebstähle und Kämpfe sowie die Taten tapferer Männer herauf. Die* Moran *werden bei ihren Aktivitäten von den jungen Mädchen beobachtet (rechts oben), geben jedoch vor, die Blicke der Frauen nicht zu bemerken.*

🇫🇷 *Les* moran *sont très liés l'un à l'autre et se partagent tout. D'après les traditions maasais, ils ne peuvent jamais manger seuls, et sont toujours vus en groupes (ci-dessus). Durant les années passées dans le* manyatta, *les* moran *laissent pousser leurs cheveux et consacrent beaucoup de temps à les tresser et à les colorer (ci-contre, en bas à gauche). A la tombée du jour, les* moran *souvent s'adonnent à l'*adumu, *une danse caractéristique (ci-contre, en bas à droite). Cette danse, ainsi que les chants qui l'accompagnent, rappellent des événements légendaires. Les jeunes filles observent de près les faits et gestes des* moran *(ci-contre, en haut), alors que ceux-ci prétendent ne rien remarquer.*

The modern age has curtailed many of the traditional duties of the moran. Lion hunting was a popular test of bravery in the past. A particularly brave morani would be awarded the lion's mane headdress, or olawaru, after the hunt. Cattle-raiding expeditions were also common. In battle, the ostrich feather headdress, or enkuraru (right), was worn as its added height gave the morani a psychological advantage over the enemy. As lion hunting and cattle raiding have been officially disallowed, today moran spend much of their time in mock battles. One such game involves hurling sisal stalks at one another, and fending off the staves with their shields (opposite and inset). In another mock fray, moran (below) chase each other with leleshwa branches.

Gegen Ende des 19. Jahrhunderts galt die Löwenjagd als beliebte Mutprobe. Einem besonders mutigen Morani wird nach der Jagd ein Kopfschmuck, der aus einer Löwenmähne gemacht und Olawaru genannt wird, überreicht. Im Kampf trug der Morani einst einen Kopfschmuck aus Straußenfedern, den Enkuraru (rechts); der Krieger erschien dadurch größer und fühlte sich somit dem Feind überlegen. Da Löwenjagd und Viehdiebstahl offiziell nicht mehr zugelassen sind, vertreiben sich die Moran heute mit Scheinkämpfen die Zeit. In einem dieser Spiele bewerfen sich die Gegner mit Sisalstöcken, die sie mit ihren Schildern abwehren (links und Einsatz). In einer anderen gespielten Kampfszene verfolgen sich die jungen Krieger (unten) gegenseitig mit Leleshwa-Zweigen.

A la fin du dix-neuvième siècle, la chasse au lion était une populaire épreuve de bravoure. Un morani qui s'y distinguait recevait alors la crinière du lion, ou olawaru, après la chasse. En combat, le morani porte la coiffe de plumes d'autruche ou enkuraru (à droite), sa hauteur supplémentaire lui donnant un avantage psychologique sur l'ennemi. De nos jours, la chasse au lion et les rafles de bétail étant interdites, les moran passent le temps dans des combats simulés. Un de ces jeux consiste à se lancer des perches de sisal que les participants doivent parer avec leurs boucliers (ci-contre et en cartouche). Dans un autre, les moran se pourchassent l'un l'autre avec des branches de leleshwa (en bas).

At the eunoto ceremony, the senior warriors graduate to junior elders. A wind instrument (below), made from the horn of a greater kudu, summons the moran to the eunoto. Called by the horn, the moran arrive in full regalia (opposite top right), their heads coloured in red ochre, and wearing lion mane and ostrich feather headdresses (opposite top left). From all over Maasailand people gather to take part in the ceremony (opposite bottom).

Bei der Eunoto-Feier werden die älteren Krieger zu rangniedrigen Ältesten ernannt. Ein Blasinstrument, das aus dem Horn des Großen Kudus gefertigt wurde (unten), ruft die Moran zum Fest. Die Krieger erscheinen in vollem Staat (ganz rechts): Die Haare sind mit rotem Ocker gefärbt, und sie tragen einen Kopfschmuck aus Löwenmähne und Straußenfedern (rechts). Aus dem ganzen Land kommen die Massai, um an dieser Feier teilzunehmen (rechts unten).

Lors de l'eunoto, les guerriers vétérans deviennent 'novices anciens'. Un instrument à vent, fait de la corne d'un kudu (ci-dessous), convoque les moran à l'eunoto. Ils arrivent dans leurs plus beaux atours (ci-contre, en haut à droite), la tête couverte d'ocre rouge, et portant des coiffes de plumes d'autruche et de crinières de lions (ci-contre, en haut à gauche). On vient de partout en Maasailand pour participer à la cérémonie (ci-contre, en bas).

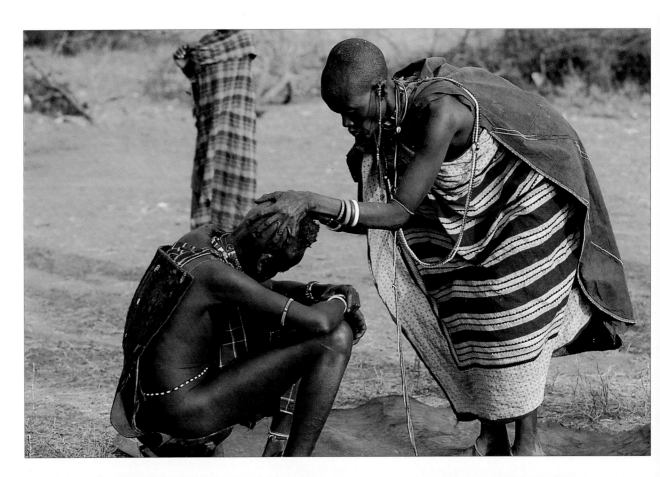

The morani's *head is shaved by his mother, symbolically severing his ties with the* warriorhood *(opposite top).* Women construct the central ceremonial edifice of the eunoto, *the* osingira *(opposite bottom). The women work hard to complete the structure and plaster the frame with cow dung and mud. Within the* osingira, *the main rituals of the* eunoto *are performed by the* laibon. *From a combination of built-up tension, hyperventilation and drugs extracted from tree bark and roots, a* morani *passes into a state of trance, known as* a-push *(above). The* morani *is led away by relatives until the trance has subsided (right).*

Die Mutter rasiert dem Morani *den Kopf und trennt ihn dadurch symbolisch von seinem Status als Krieger (links oben). Die Frauen errichten das* Osingira *(links unten), das Hauptgebäude der* Eunoto-*Zeremonie. Im* Osingira *werden die wichtigsten Rituale von einem* Laibon *durchgeführt. Eine Kombination von aufgestauter Spannung, Hyperventilation und aus Baumrinde und Wurzeln hergestellten Drogen versetzt den* Morani *in einen Trancezustand,* a-push *(oben) genannt. Er wird von seinen Verwandten umsorgt, bis er aus der Trance erwacht (rechts).*

La mère du morani *lui rase la tête, coupant ainsi symboliquement ses liens avec sa vie de guerrier (ci-contre, en haut). Les femmes construisent l'*osingira, *l'édifice central pour la cérémonie de l'*eunoto *(ci-contre, en bas). Elles travaillent dur pour achever l'armature et la recouvrir de bouse et de boue. A l'intérieur de l'*osingira, *les rites principaux de l'*eunoto *sont exécutés par le* laibon. *Un mélange de tension accumulée, d'hyperventilation et de drogues extraites d'écorces et de racines, font passer un* morani *dans un état de transe qui est appelé* a-push *(ci-dessus). Le jeune* morani, *supporté par sa famille, est emmené en attendant qu'il se calme (à droite).*

After the **eunoto** participants have had their heads shaved by their mothers and smeared with red ochre, the men then gather together to sing and dance (above). During the **eunoto** ceremony, several oxen are slaughtered and ceremonial feasting takes place. The meat from the oxen is roasted and distributed to the elders, women and participants (opposite bottom). The hide of a sacrificial black ox is pegged out by prominent women in the community. Each woman hammers in a peg for each of her warrior sons. The hide is then cut into thin strips. Graduates line up to receive a ring of hide (left), a sign that they have passed the judgment of the elders. The elders blow milk over the squatting junior elders as a final blessing (opposite top).

Nachdem den **Eunoto**-Teilnehmern von ihren Müttern die Köpfe rasiert und mit rotem Ocker eingerieben wurden, versammeln sie sich zum Singen und Tanzen (oben). Während der Feier schlachtet man Ochsen und hält ein Festessen ab. Das Fleisch wird gebraten und verteilt (ganz links). Die Haut eines schwarzen Ochsen wird von den angesehenen Frauen der Gemeinschaft aufgespannt. Jede Frau hämmert für einen jeden ihrer Söhne, der zu den Kriegern gehört, einen Stift ein. Danach wird die Haut in dünne Streifen geschnitten. Die **Eunoto**-Absolventen stellen sich in einer Reihe auf und erhalten einen Lederreif (links) zum Zeichen dafür, daß sie nach dem Urteil der Ältesten die Prüfung bestanden haben. Zum abschließenden Segen gießen die Stammesältesten Milch über die rangniedrigeren Ältesten (gegenüber oben).

Après que les participants à l'**eunoto** ont eu la tête rasée par leur mère et recouverte d'ocre rouge, les hommes se rassemblent pour danser et chanter (ci-dessus). Pendant la cérémonie de l'**eunoto**, plusieurs boeufs sont abattus et on participe à des réjouissances cérémonielles. La viande est grillée et distribuée parmi les anciens, les femmes et les participants (ci-contre, en bas). La peau d'un boeuf noir sacrifié est étendue et fixée avec des piquets par les femmes importantes de la communauté. Pour chaque fils guerrier, les mères enfoncent un piquet. La peau est alors coupée en minces lanières. Les nouveaux guerriers se mettent en file pour recevoir un anneau de peau (à gauche), indiquant qu'ils ont satisfait les anciens. Comme dernière bénédiction, les anciens aspergent du lait sur les nouveaux élus accroupis (ci-contre, en haut).

The eunoto *ceremony is an infrequent occurrence in the Maasai calendar and occurs at intervals of about 15 years. Within the* manyatta *49 dwellings are constructed surrounding the* osingira*. The* eunoto *ceremony attracts large crowds of spectators who make the most of the occasion by dressing up (below). Between the major events much singing and dancing takes place (right). Maasai men frequently take part in* adumu *dances (opposite left and right). The men form a circle and sing a deep rhythmic song. One or two of the men dance in the centre of the circle, leaping up and down, their bodies held rigid and their faces set in fierce concentration.*

Die Eunoto-*Zeremonie der* Massai *findet im allgemeinen nur alle 15 Jahre statt. Innerhalb der* Manyatta *werden 49 Hütten um das* Osingira *errichtet. Die Zeremonie zieht Scharen von Zuschauern an, die die Gelegenheit nutzen, um ihre besten Gewänder und den* Perlenschmuck *anzulegen (unten). Zwischen den einzelnen Ereignissen wird viel getanzt und gesungen (rechts).* Massaimänner *nehmen oft an den* Adumu-Tänzen *teil (ganz rechts und rechts Mitte). Die Männer bilden einen Kreis und singen in tiefer Stimme rhythmische Lieder. Ein oder zwei Männer tanzen in der Kreismitte und springen mit steifem Körper und angespanntem Gesicht auf und ab.*

L'eunoto *n'est pas un événement très courant et n'est célébré qu'une fois tous les 15 ans. Dans l'enceinte du* manyatta*, on construit 49 habitations en cercle, autour de l'*osingira*. L'*eunoto *attire une foule nombreuse de spectateurs qui marquent cette occasion en se parant de tissus et de perles (ci-dessous). On chante et on danse beaucoup entre les différentes parties de la cérémonie (à droite). Les hommes maasais participent dans la danse de l'*adumu *(ci-contre, à gauche et à droite). Ils forment un cercle et chantent en cadence. Un ou deux hommes dansent au centre du cercle en bondissant, le corps et le visage figés par la concentration.*

In Maasai society, pubescent girls are obliged to undergo an operation that involves the removal of the clitoris. The operation is usually done by a member of another tribe and is performed inside the dwelling belonging to the girl's mother. As the girl is led away to recover there is much celebration. Women dressed in all their finery (above) gather in the enkang to take part in the festivities. The women dance and sing praises to the girl (opposite bottom). After the operation, the girls paint their faces with white chalk, dress in black and wear a circular beaded band around their heads (opposite top).

In der Massaigesellschaft werden pubertierende Mädchen einer Operation unterzogen, bei der die Klitoris entfernt wird. Den Eingriff führt man in der Hütte der Mutter des Mädchens durch. Wenn das Mädchen zur Genesung weggeführt wird, findet eine große Feier statt. Die zurechtgemachten Frauen (oben) versammeln sich in der Enkang, um an den Feierlichkeiten teilzunehmen. Sie tanzen und singen Loblieder auf das Mädchen (rechts). Nach der Operation bemalen die Mädchen ihre Gesichter mit weißer Kreide, kleiden sich in Schwarz und tragen ein Perlenband um den Kopf (rechts oben).

Dans la société maasai, les jeunes filles pubères subissent l'ablation du clitoris. L'opération est faite dans l'habitation appartenant à la mère de la jeune fille. Alors qu'elle est emmenée pour guérir, l'événement est marqué par des festivités. Des femmes, parées de leurs plus beaux atours (ci-dessus) se rassemblent dans l'enkang avant de participer aux réjouissances. Elles dansent et chantent des louanges à la jeune fille (ci-contre, en bas). Après l'opération, les jeunes filles se couvrent le visage de craie blanche, se vêtent de noir et portent un bandeau de perles autour de la tête (ci-contre, en haut).

After the initiation, which marks the passage to womanhood, the young women wear distinctive headdresses decorated with cowrie shells to symbolize fertility (below). During the six-week recovery period the young women are not permitted to talk to men or strangers. Long beaded tassels (opposite top right and bottom) or chains (opposite top left), forming part of their headdresses, partially obscure their faces, symbolic of their exclusion. During this period they are known as ormaisen, or 'girls in healing'. After completing this initiation, Maasai women are allowed to marry.

Nach der Initiation, durch die das Mädchen zur Frau wird, trägt die junge Frau einen kunstvollen Kopfschmuck, der mit Kaurimuscheln, dem Symbol der Fruchtbarkeit, verziert ist (unten). Während der sechswöchigen Genesungszeit ist es den jungen Frauen, Ormaisen, nicht gestattet, mit Männern oder Fremden zu sprechen. Die langen, am Kopfschmuck angebrachten Perlenquasten (links und links unten) oder Ketten (ganz links) verdecken die Gesichter zum Zeichen der Ausgeschlossenheit. Erst nach dieser Zeremonie ist es einer jungen Frau erlaubt zu heiraten.

Après l'initiation qui marque leur changement de statut, les jeunes femmes portent des coiffes spéciales décorées de cauris symbolisant la fertilité (ci-dessous). Durant leurs six semaines de convalescence, il est interdit aux jeunes femmes, ou ormaisen, de parler aux hommes ou aux inconnus. Comme symbole de leur exclusion elles ont le visage partiellement caché par de longs pompons (ci-contre, en haut à droite et en bas) ou des chaînes (ci-contre, en haut à gauche) couvertes de perles, faisant partie de leur coiffe. Après avoir achevé cette initiation les femmes maasais sont autorisées à se marier.

After the eunoto *ceremony Maasai men are able to lead a more settled life. One of a junior elder's most urgent concerns is marriage, and gifts are taken to a prospective bride's parents. Once the offer of marriage has been accepted, the prospective groom (opposite right) will offer as many gifts as he can afford. On the day of the wedding, the members of the bride's family put on their finest necklaces, and paint their faces with red ochre (above). The young bride is carefully dressed in the softest skins by her mother (right). As she leaves her* enkang *the bride is blessed by her father (opposite left). Expressing great sorrow, the bride then leaves the familiar comforts of her* enkang *behind.*

Nach der Eunoto-Feier *können die Massaimänner ein geregelteres Leben führen. Da die Ehe eines der dringendsten Anliegen eines rangniedrigen Ältesten ist, bringt er den Eltern der ausgewählten Braut Geschenke. Wird das Heiratsangebot angenommen, so schickt der zukünftige Bräutigam (ganz rechts) so viele Geschenke, wie er sich leisten kann. Am Hochzeitstag legen die Familienmitglieder der Braut (oben) ihre edelsten Halsketten an und bemalen sich die Gesichter mit rotem Ocker. Die junge Braut wird von ihrer Mutter sorgfältig in weiches Leder gekleidet (rechts). Beim Verlassen des* Enkang *segnet der Vater seine wegziehende Tochter (oben Mitte). Unter Wehklagen läßt die Braut ihr vertrautes Elternheim hinter sich.*

Après la cérémonie de l'eunoto *les hommes maasais peuvent poursuivre une vie plus normale. Maintenant, une des préoccupations majeures du novice ancien sera le mariage, et des cadeaux sont présentés aux parents de la future épouse. Une fois que l'offre de mariage a été acceptée, le futur marié (ci-contre, à droite) fera autant de cadeaux qu'il puisse se permettre. Le jour du mariage, les membres de la famille de la mariée (ci-dessus) porteront leurs plus beaux colliers et se couvriront le visage d'ocre rouge. La jeune mariée est revêtue avec soin par sa mère des peaux les plus délicates (à droite). Alors qu'elle quitte l'enkang, son père la bénit (ci-contre, à gauche). Pleine de tristesse, la mariée abandonne alors le bien-être familier de son* enkang.

The young bride is escorted by the groom and his best man to her new home (left). As she proceeds, the bride (below) walks slowly, her eyes focused on the path. Upon arrival at the groom's enkang, the bride is welcomed by the women (opposite top). The bride then enters her future mother-in-law's dwelling and remains there until the wedding takes place (opposite bottom).

Die junge Braut wird vom Bräutigam und den Brautzeugen zu ihrem neuen Heim begleitet (links). Sie geht dabei langsam und hält die Augen auf den Pfad gerichtet (unten). Bei ihrer Ankunft in der Enkang *des Bräutigams wird sie von den Frauen des Hauses begrüßt (rechts). Die Braut betritt dann die Hütte ihrer zukünftigen Schwiegermutter und bleibt dort, bis die Hochzeit stattfindet (rechts unten).*

La jeune mariée est escortée par son époux et son témoin vers sa nouvelle demeure (à gauche). En chemin, la mariée marche lentement, les yeux fixés par terre (ci-dessous). En arrivant à l'enkang de son époux, elle est accueillie par les femmes (ci-contre, en haut). La mariée pénètre alors dans l'habitation de sa future belle-mère, où elle restera jusqu'au moment du mariage (ci-contre, en bas).

Several Maasai families establish their homes within the circular enkang settlement, guarded by a thorn-branch hedge erected to deter lions and other predators (opposite top left). Maasai women construct the low dwellings around the perimeter of the settlement, allowing space in the centre for cattle to be penned at night. A Maasai elder (opposite bottom) may have several wives. His first wife constructs a separate dwelling on the right of the entrance leading into the enkang; the second wife to the left. Apart from being responsible for building and maintaining the dwellings, Maasai women milk the cows and gather firewood (opposite top right). As the site chosen for the enkang has to be level, the settlement may be some distance from the nearest watercourse (above), where a young boy and a warrior draw water in a cow-hide container.

Mehrere Massaifamilien gründen ihr Heim innerhalb der kreisförmigen Enkang-Siedlung, die von einer Dornenhecke umgeben ist, um Raubtiere fernzuhalten (ganz links oben). Die Massaifrauen errichten die niedrigen Hütten am äußersten Rand der Siedlung, so daß in der Mitte genügend Platz bleibt, um dort das Vieh nachts einzupferchen. Ein Massaiältester (links unten) kann mehrere Frauen haben. Seine erste Frau baut eine Hütte auf der rechten Seite des Enkang-Eingangs, die zweite Frau eine auf der linken. Die Massaifrauen sind für den Bau und die Instandhaltung der Hütten verantwortlich, außerdem melken sie die Kühe und sammeln Feuerholz (links oben). Der nächste Wasserlauf kann weit von der Siedlung entfernt sein (oben), aus dem ein kleiner Junge und ein Krieger mit einem Gefäß aus Kuhleder Wasser schöpfen.

Plusieurs familles maasais s'établissent dans l'enceinte circulaire de l'enkang, protégées par une haie d'épines érigée afin de décourager les lions et autres animaux sauvages (ci-contre, en haut à gauche). Les femmes construisent des habitations basses autour du périmètre du campement, laissant un espace au centre pour y garder le bétail durant la nuit. Un ancien Maasai (ci-contre, en bas) peut avoir plusieurs épouses. Sa première femme construit une habitation séparée à droite de l'entrée de l'enkang; sa seconde femme, à gauche. En plus d'être responsables pour les bâtiments et l'entretien des habitations, les femmes traient aussi les vaches et ramassent le bois à brûler (ci-contre, en haut à droite). Le campement peut être à quelque distance du point d'eau le plus proche (ci-dessus). Ici, deux Maasais remplissent un récipient.

Cattle ownership takes centre stage in the economic life of the Maasai people. As if they were children, each animal in a herd is known individually and each animal is nurtured accordingly. At times, young animals (left) are housed within the dwellings at night to protect them from the cold. A household head of moderate wealth will own a herd of 50 cattle. Cows are milked by women (opposite top left), and milk forms a crucial part of the Maasai's diet. Each Maasai clan has its own distinctive brand for marking cattle, but a favourite bull (opposite top right) may be decorated with elaborate markings. In the Maa language over 30 nouns describe cattle according to their coloration and horn shape (opposite bottom). On the grassy plains of the Mara, Maasai cattle graze near a herd of plains zebra (below).

Im wirtschaftlichen Leben der Massai nimmt der Viehbesitz eine zentrale Stellung ein. Der Besitzer kennt und pflegt jedes einzelne Tier in der Herde fast wie ein Kind. Bisweilen werden Jungtiere (links) nachts in den Hütten untergebracht, um sie vor der Kälte zu schützen. Ein wohl-habender Haushaltsvorstand besitzt eine Herde von rund 50 Rindern. Die Kühe werden von den Frauen gemolken (rechts), und die Milch spielt in der Ernährung der Massai eine wichtige Rolle. Eine jede Massaisippe verfügt über ein unverkennbares Brandzeichen zur Kennzeichnung der Rinder; für das Leittier (ganz rechts) wird oft ein besonderes Kennzei-chen entworfen, mit dem es gebrandmarkt wird. In der Maa-Sprache gibt es mehr als 30 Substantive, die die Rinder je nach Färbung und Form der Hörner beschreiben (rechts unten). Auf den Ebenen der Mara grasen die Viehherden der Massai unweit einer Herde Steppenzebras (unten).

La possession de bétail est au centre de la vie économique des Maasai. Dans un troupeau, chaque animal est connu individuellement et choyé, comme s'il s'agissait d'un enfant. Il arrive que des animaux passent la nuit à l'intérieur des habitations (à gauche) pour les protéger du froid. Un chef de ménage aux moyens modérés aura un troupeau de 50 têtes de bétail. Les femmes traient les vaches (ci-contre, en haut à gauche), et le lait joue un rôle primordial dans le régime alimentaire des Maasais. Chaque clan maasai a sa propre marque pour identifier le bétail, mais un taureau préféré (ci-contre, en haut à droite) pourra être décoré par des ornements complexes. La langue maa possède plus de 30 mots décrivant le bétail d'après la couleur et la forme des cornes (ci-contre, en bas). Dans les plaines herbeuses de Mara, le bétail maasai broute près d'un troupeau de zèbres (ci-dessous).

After completing their daily responsibilities, Maasai women gather to thread beaded necklaces and bracelets (above). Both men and women wear beaded decorations. Ear ornaments (opposite) may be worn only by a married woman with a son who has been circumcised. A narrow decorated leather belt supports the hide scabbard of the short sword carried by the moran (inset). These belts are often made more attractive by attaching a beaded design sewn on a leather base to the back of the belt (left).

Nach getaner Arbeit treffen sich die Frauen, um Perlen für Halsketten und Armbänder aufzureihen (oben). Sowohl Männer als auch Frauen legen Perlenschmuck an. Ohrschmuck (ganz links) darf nur von einer verheirateten Frau, die einen beschnittenen Sohn hat, getragen werden. Ein schmaler, verzierter Ledergurt enthält die Lederscheide für das kurze Schwert, das die Moran tragen (Einsatz). Sie werden oft durch ein Perlenmuster verschönert, das auf Leder genäht und hinten am Gürtel angebracht wird (links).

Après avoir terminé leurs corvées quotidiennes, les femmes se rassemblent pour enfiler des colliers et des bracelets (ci-dessus). Hommes et femmes portent des ornements de perles. Les femmes ne peuvent se parer les oreilles (ci-contre) que si elles sont mariées et ont un fils circoncis. Une étroite ceinture de cuir décoré supporte le fourreau de peau de la courte épée portée par les moran (en cartouche). Ces ceintures sont souvent décorées avec un motif en perles cousues sur du cuir à l'arrière de la ceinture (à gauche).

Junior elders (opposite top) *dance to an audience of children. Junior elders are careful to show respect to the senior elders (below),* who *assume responsibility for their mentorship. All important decisions affecting the community are taken by the senior elders in their council of elders, the* enkiguena. *Elders are noted for their articulate speeches, and their love of parables and allegory. Status is based on the wisdom of the elder (opposite bottom)* and not on wealth.

Die rangniedrigeren Ältesten (links) tanzen vor einem Kinderpublikum. Sie sind darauf bedacht, den Stammesältesten, die sich als Mentoren für sie verantwortlich fühlen, Respekt zu erweisen (unten). Alle wichtigen, die Gemeinschaft betreffenden Entscheidungen werden von den ranghöheren Ältesten im Ältestenrat, dem Enkiguena, getroffen. Prestige erwerben sich die Ältesten (links unten) durch Weisheit und nicht durch Reichtum.

De novices anciens (ci-contre, en haut) dansent devant une audience composée d'enfants. Les novices font montre de respect envers les aînés (ci-dessous). Toutes décisions touchant la communauté sont prises par les aînés, dans leur conseil des anciens, l'enkiguena. Les anciens sont connus pour la clarté de leurs discours et leur amour de l'usage de la langue. Le prestige d'un ancien (ci-contre, en bas) est basé sur sa sagesse et non sur ses possessions.

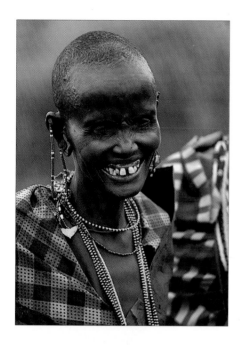

For the senior elder, old age represents the passage from one stage to another. Many of their former tasks are taken over by the younger sets. Senior elders spend much of the day in contemplation (top right). The most revered of the elders is the laibon, a spiritual leader and healer (above). Here the laibon, dressed in animal fur, instructs his sons as he petitions the ancestors for a prophecy. For Maasai women (top left and opposite), old age is a time for consolidating and continuing their influence within the enkang.

Der ranghohe Älteste tritt mit zunehmendem Alter in ein neues Stadium ein. Viele seiner Aufgaben werden von Jüngeren übernommen. Die Ältesten verbringen den Tag in besinnlicher Zurückgezogenheit (ganz oben rechts). Der Laibon (oben) ist geistiger Führer und Heiler, der große Achtung genießt. Der Laibon erteilt seinen Söhnen Aufträge, während er die Vorfahren um eine Prophezeiung anruft. Ältere Massaifrauen (ganz oben links und gegenüber) wollen ihre Stellung in der Enkang bewahren.

Pour l'ancien aîné, le vieil âge représente la transition d'un stade à l'autre. Les aînés passent la plus grande partie de la journée en contemplation (en haut à droite). Le plus honoré des anciens est le laibon, un maître spirituel et guérisseur (ci-dessus). Ici, un laibon vêtu de peaux de bêtes, instruit ses fils alors qu'il s'adresse aux ancêtres pour demander une prophétie. Pour les femmes maasais (en haut à gauche, et ci-contre), le vieil âge est le moment d'affermir et d'étendre leur influence dans l'enkang.

🇬🇧 *Although the Maasai still cling to their age-old traditions, modern influences are increasingly impacting on their culture. A package tour to the wildlife reserves usually includes a visit to a Maasai* enkang *(left). Although the entrance fee levied is paid to an elder, Maasai women trade necklaces, bracelets and gourds to tourists for hard currency (opposite top left and opposite top right). Another modern influence is Western-based education. The young man dressed in Western clothes (above) was selected by the elders to attend school so that he may later become the tribal scribe. And Western dress (right) is worn by some Maasai.*

🇩🇪 *Obwohl die Massai noch immer an ihren jahrhundertealten Traditionen festhalten, üben moderne Einflüsse eine immer stärkere Wirkung auf ihre Kultur aus. Eine Pauschalreise in die Naturreservate umfaßt gewöhnlich einen Besuch in einer* Enkang *(links). Die Eintrittsgebühr wird einem der Ältesten übergeben, und Massaifrauen verkaufen ihren Schmuck und Kürbisflaschen gegen harte Währung an die Touristen (ganz links oben und links oben). Ein weiterer Einfluß der Moderne ist eine Ausbildung nach westlichem Vorbild. Der junge Mann (oben) wurde ausgewählt, die Schule zu besuchen, um einmal der Schreiber des Stammes zu werden. Vor allem in Städten tragen Massai westliche Kleidung (rechts).*

🇫🇷 *Bien que les Maasais s'accrochent à leurs anciennes traditions, l'influence du monde moderne a un effet sur leur culture. Un voyage organisé dans les réserves naturelles comprend généralement une visite dans un* enkang *maasai (à gauche). Bien que le prix de l'entrée soit versé à un ancien, les femmes maasais vendent des colliers et bracelets aux touristes, en échange de devises fortes (ci-contre, en haut à gauche et à droite). Une autre influence de la vie moderne est l'éducation occidentale. Le jeune homme (ci-dessus) fut désigné par les anciens pour aller à l'école, afin de devenir le scribe de la tribu. D'autres Maasais eux aussi, s'habillent à la mode occidentale (à droite), en particulier dans des villes comme Narok.*

For centuries the Maasai have been tenacious defenders of their pastoral lifestyle and culture. With the arrival of British rule the Maasai lost much of their power and territory. Today the Maasai represent a small minority amongst the expanding populations of Kenya and Tanzania. Confined to the savannas of southern Kenya and northern Tanzania, the Maasai preserve a culture that is at times in conflict with the nation states that now divide their territory. Whether Maasai culture can survive the future will ultimately depend on the needs of an expanding population, and the way in which scant natural resources are divided.

Seit Jahrhunderten verteidigen die Massai beharrlich ihren Lebensstil und ihre Kultur als Hirtenvolk. Unter britischer Herrschaft verloren sie einen Großteil ihrer Macht und ihres Landes. Heute bilden die Massai eine kleine Minderheit unter der wachsenden Bevölkerung Kenias und Tansanias. Die ausschließlich in den Savannen Südkenias und Nordtansanias lebenden Massai erhalten eine Kultur, die zuweilen mit den Staaten, die sich nun ihr Territorium teilen, in Konflikt gerät. Ob die Kultur der Massai weiterbestehen kann, hängt letztlich davon ab, wie sich die Bedürfnisse einer wachsenden Bevölkerung entwickeln und wie die knappen Güter der Natur aufgeteilt werden.

Pendant des siècles, les Maasai ont défendu avec ténacité leur culture et leur mode de vie pastorale. L'arrivée des Anglais leur fit perdre beaucoup de leurs pouvoirs et de leur territoire. De nos jours, les Maasai ne représentent qu'une petite minorité parmi les populations croissantes du Kenya et de Tanzanie. Restreints aux savanes du sud du Kenya et du nord de la Tanzanie, ils protègent une culture qui de temps à autre est en conflit avec les états qui divisent leur territoire. La survie de la culture maasai dépendra finalement des besoins d'une population croissante et de la façon dont seront réparties les maigres ressources de la région.

Struik Publishers
(a division of New Holland Publishing (South Africa) (Pty) Ltd)
Cornelis Struik House, 80 McKenzie Street, Cape Town 8001
Website: *www.struik.co.za*

New Holland Publishing is a member of the Johnnic Publishing Group
Log on to our photographic website *www.imagesofafrica.co.za* for an
African experience

First published 1995
4 6 8 10 9 7 5
Copyright © in published edition: Struik Publishers 1995
Text © Michael Brett 1995
Map © Globetrotter Travel Maps 1995

Managing editor: Mariëlle Renssen
Editor: Christine Riley
Design manager: Petal Palmer
Designer: Peter Bosman
German translation: Regina Bailey
German editor: Bettina Kaufmann
French translation: Jean-Paul Houssière
French editors: Christine Riley and Bettina Kaufmann

Typesetting by Struik DTP, Cape Town
Reproduction by Hirt & Carter (Cape) (Pty) Ltd
Printed and bound by Kyodo Printing Co (Singapore) Pte Ltd

ISBN 1 86825 763 0

Photographs © individual photographers and/or their agents (1995) as listed below:

Daryl and Sharna Balfour/SIL: *front cover (inset bottom), back cover, p. 3;*
Carol Beckwith: *pp. 5, 6 (top right & bottom), 12, 18 (inset), 19 (bottom),*
25 (top),32 (top & bottom), 33 (left), 34 (top), 36 (top right), 40, 41 (top & bottom right),
44(top right & bottom); **Peter Blackwell:** *pp. 6 (top left); 14, 15, 16, 21 (top right),*
38(top), 39 (top left), 46 (top left); **Camerapix:** *pp. 4 (top), 9 (top), 10 (bottom left),*
19(top), 21 (top left & bottom), 22 (bottom), 23 (top & bottom), 24 (top & bottom),
25 (bottom), 30 (top right & bottom), 34 (bottom), 40 (right), 42 (bottom), 43;
Peter Lamberti: *p. 7;* **Peter and Stefania Lamberti:** *p. 9 (bottom right);*
Nigel Pavitt:front cover, pp. 1, 13 (bottom), 18, 20, 31, 37, 48; **Mitch Reardon:** *pp. 9*
(bottomleft), 10 (bottom right), 12 (inset), 13 (top), 17 (top, bottom right & bottom left),
26 (bottom), 30 (top left), 35 (top & bottom), 36 (bottom), 38 (bottom), 39 (top right),
42 (top), 44 (top left), 45, 46 (top right & bottom), 47 (top & bottom);
Dave Richards: *front cover (inset top), pp. 8, 10 (top), 27 (left & right), 28,29 (bottom);*
Anup Shah/ABPL: *p. 4 (bottom);* **David Steele/Photo Access:** *p. 39 (bottom);*
Clive Ward: *pp. 11, 26 (top), 33 (right), 36 (top left);*
Duncan Willetts/Camerapix: *p. 22 (top).*